hope**bl♥oms**

Plant a Seed, Harvest a Dream

Written by Mamadou Wade
and the youth of Hope Blooms

Foreword by Arlene Dickinson
of *Dragons' Den*

NIMBUS
PUBLISHING
NIMBUS.CA

Nimbus Publishing Limited
3660 Strawberry Hill Street, Halifax, NS, B3K 5A9
(902) 455-4286 nimbus.ca

Printed and bound in Canada

Editor: Whitney Moran
Design: Kate Westphal
Cover images: Snickerdoodle Photography (top; bottom left); remainder courtesy Hope Blooms

Photos on pages 22 and 106 by Snickerdoodle Photography
Food photography on pages 58,61, 63, 73, 78, 81, 86, 89, 93, 96, 98 by Chelsea Demings Photos
Photos on pages 40, 49 by Brinton Photography
All other images provided courtesy of Hope Blooms

Library and Archives Canada Cataloguing in Publication

Wade, Mamadou, 1997-, author
Hope Blooms : plant a seed, harvest a dream / written byMamadou Wade and the youth of Hope Blooms ; foreword by Arlene Dickinson of Dragons' Den.

ISBN 978-1-77108-695-0 (softcover)

1. Social entrepreneurship—Nova Scotia--Halifax. 2. New business enterprises—Nova Scotia—Halifax. 3. Produce trade—Nova Scotia—Halifax. 4. Problem youth—Nova Scotia—Halifax. 5. Mentoring—Nova Scotia—Halifax.
I. Title.

HD60.5.C22H35 2018   338'.0409716225   C2018-902907-2

Nimbus Publishing acknowledges the financial support for its publishing activities from the Government of Canada, the Canada Council for the Arts, and from the Province of Nova Scotia. We are pleased to work in partnership with the Province of Nova Scotia to develop and promote our creative industries for the benefit of all Nova Scotians.

 Chef Tash

 Folayemi Boboye

 Shaani Singh

 Mamadou Wade

 Jill Martin

 Bocar Wade

 Sarina Piercy

 Alenne Adekayoda

 Kylee Hendricks

MIX
Paper from responsible sources
FSC® C016245

"Even
After
All this time
The Sun never says to the Earth,
'You owe me.'
Look
What happens
With a love like that,
It lights the whole sky."
–Hafiz

Contents

Celebrating our gala alongside Arlene Dickinson (2017).

Foreword

Almost a decade ago, I was introduced to an organization called Hope Blooms. The organization had made the long trip from Halifax to Toronto to pitch their community project on *Dragons' Den*. The project, taken at face value, was an urban food garden that produced organic food and salad dressing. In reality, it was so much more.

This book is the story of how a visionary community leader transformed an abandoned plot of land into a source of education, employment, and ultimately empowerment for inner-city and at-risk youth. It's the story of how all children have the strength and ability to overcome personal hardships to become agents of transformational change in their own lives and in their communities, when given the opportunity.

Today, that small plot of weed-infested urban land is home to four thousand square feet of organic food gardens and an award-winning off-the-grid greenhouse designed by one of the Hope Blooms participants. Youth members grow food for their community, and a small commercial kitchen turns those vegetables into salad dressing. Hope Blooms embodies impactful social entrepreneurship.

The lessons shared in this book extend far beyond urban gardening. They are lessons in what can be achieved when the disenfranchised are empowered. It is the story of the extraordinary social and economic impact a single child can have on their community, and on their country, when they are given *hope*. Welcome to ten years in the life of Hope Blooms.

–Arlene Dickinson, of *Dragons' Den*

In a world where our actions are constantly determined by the potential of monetary compensation, Hope Blooms has created a more powerful, impactful currency: hope. Acting for the greater good of everyone. Love trumps all; unity is an unstoppable force that we believe can pierce a resistant defined as immovable.

Inspiring others to have the courage to propel their dreams forward cannot be given a fiscal value. Hope Blooms. Plant a seed, harvest a dream.

Introducing Hope Blooms

"You may think I'm small, but I have a universe inside my mind."
–Yoko Ono

I chose my career path as a dietitian because of my desire to work with people, with a focus on health. To me, food was fundamental. Food impacts every aspect of our mind, body, emotional and spiritual well-being. Food connects, builds, strengthens, nurtures, brings joy, and touches the essence of who we are: our identity, our culture, our childhood memories, big and small life moments, good times and bad. As a dietitian working in inner-city health, year after year I witnessed the impact of not having access to healthy foods, not being able to afford fresh fruits and vegetables, not having the means to purchase what was recommended to treat, let alone prevent, chronic illness. I have witnessed the social exclusion, lack of support networks and, generally, what I saw as racialized poverty.

I had attended a lecture where a renowned physician stated that he did not believe in hope; that hope gave a false feeling that things would work out, and he observed that life does not always get better. This haunted me for months. I thought, What if we could see hope, could feel hope come to life before our eyes? What if we could create a place where hope bloomed right before us?

And I thought of children in the North End community to be brilliant and beautiful. I thought, What if they were able to grow up being change makers, and disrupt the cycle of poverty? This, to me, meant starting from the ground up: building relationships with our earth, with growing their own organic food, feeding the community, cooking together, including all cultures and celebrating our roots, and building big futures through their own food-based social enterprise that grows a love for education and means of pursuing this, through scholarships. It was a dream, and I had no idea if it was possible, but the children thought it was possible and began to dream a dream big enough for everyone to share in…a place where hope does bloom. It has not been a smooth, easy, or short journey; there have been many struggles and

obstacles, and many ups and downs. To me, it is all sacred, and we belong to each other.

Jakub and Erica getting
the plant perspective.

☆

When children feel empowered to come together to create a positive impact in the community in which they live; when they imagine possibilities and work to create the extraordinary from nothing; when they plant their seeds, nurture the soil, and harvest dreams big enough for all to share in; when they define success by not only finding their joy, but by the joy they bring to others, we all share in this sacred journey and hold the universe in our minds and hearts.

(FACING PAGE) Jurni in the dandelion
greens.

Within a context of long-term impact for generational change, children join Hope Blooms when they are five years old and graduate when they are eighteen, at which time they receive an annual scholarship funded by the proceeds of their salad-dressing social enterprise. What began with a small plot of land has grown into a youth-driven movement with over fifty youth from diverse ethnicities, building climate resilience food security environments; mentorship and leadership development in social innovation and experiential education; and ecosystems in agriculture, culinary, arts, health, and well-being, where everyone is valued and everyone contributes.

Hope Blooms programming is carried out within a framework of inspiring excellence in our thoughts and actions and fostering culturally diverse relationships that span across generations and ethnicities. Our core education programming includes:

Youth becoming inclusive and impactful community leaders in a marginalized environment

Each year more than fifty youth grow over three thousand pounds of organic produce in and for their community; they also grow pride and a sense of belonging in community, and a social enterprise that builds brighter futures from the ground up, all while giving back to the community.

Fostering culturally relevant and collaborative ecosystems with integrity

Inclusivity and embracing diversity are core to everything we do, from welcoming new neighbours with open arms to inviting friends from all walks of life to take part in our programming. We collaborate with mentors from our local universities, community colleges, junior high and high schools, as well as many local restaurants, businesses, and organizations.

Innovation in urban agriculture education

From hands-on skill-building in agriculture to designing and operating an off-the-grid greenhouse, youth have access to a suite of non-traditional educational programming. Working with mentors, youth take the lead in environmental stewardship, and learn best practices in organic food growing, food systems, and ecosystems. Youth also participate in creating a Food Charter for the Halifax Regional Municipality and engage in meetings working towards a National Food Policy in an effort to continue the fight in ensuring better food security in our communities.

Coaction

When people come together to create a positive impact in the communities in which they live, the social determinants of health are directly impacted, particularly education, food security, social inclusion, and safety support networks. We have created a social entrepreneurial environment where people, regardless of age or socioeconomic status, can work together to build capacity and employment while giving back to the community.

For youth, there are few places where they feel they have control over anything or where they can be themselves without judgment. Hope Blooms youth are empowered to take control and actively steer the direction programming takes. In doing so, they take ownership over their contributions and are able to experience the true freedoms of their own efforts. Through hosting monthly community suppers for upwards of forty people, taking their learnings and mentoring younger youth, teaching parents and neighbours how to grow food, preparing organic soups for seniors, or donating portions of the herb-dressing proceeds to supporting other community-building efforts, these youth are learning and teaching others that the path to self-actualization is also a path to generosity.

–Jessie Jollymore, director and founder, Hope Blooms

Celebrating the harvest.

Pop up visit at one of the many Superstores that support us in carrying our dressings.

Hope Blooms Timeline

2008 We planted our first seeds in an abandoned garden plot in North End Halifax. There were nine children aged five to twelve, all of whom lived next to the garden, who joined. We grew a lot of tomatoes and all came together to make 150 bottles of salsa from ingredients we grew. We voted to give 100 percent of our proceeds to a local women's shelter. We called our business Salsamania, and our love of creating something from nothing, and then doing good in our community with monies we made, was born.

2009 We decided to grow more vegetables, take produce home to our families, and then make preserves to sell at the local farmers' market. This venture, Super Sonic Veggies, was born.

2010 We grew to include fifteen children from our community. We dug six more plots and decided to plant a few herbs to try making fresh herb dressings. We sampled at local markets.

2011 We grew to nineteen children. Together, we decided on three flavours of herb dressings to make and sell at our farmers' market. We sold all 499 bottles and used the proceeds to create a scholarship for a youth in our community.

Growing our garden and growing our business.

2013 After lots of practice, we pitched to the Dragons on CBC's hit show *Dragons' Den*. We grew to thirty youth within our program. The Canadian Armed Forces built us our first-ever greenhouse with proceeds earned from Dragon investors.

2014 Hope Blooms became a registered charity. We grew to forty children and expanded to offer family cooking classes, community kitchens, and broke a record when we grew over three thousand pounds of organic vegetables and fruits in our gardens.

2015 Build Right Nova Scotia mentored our youth and built a solar-powered, off-the-grid, award-winning greenhouse for us, next to our gardens.

2016 Mamadou Wade, our oldest youth, graduated high school, was accepted into the University of Toronto, and became first recipient of a Hope Blooms Scholarship. Our salad dressings were now being carried in Loblaws stores throughout Nova Scotia.

2017 Three more youth graduate high school and move to post secondary, all receiving yearly renewable scholarships. We grew to over fifty youth and expanded our gardens and programming to also include thirty-five local families. Broke our record with growing over four thousand pounds of organic vegetables and fruits for our community, all free.

2018 Kolade Boboye has graduated high school and been accepted into St. Francis Xavier University to study commerce. We are launching our second social enterprise, Possibili-teas, helping single mothers in Senegal. Creating positive change locally while having a global impact with 100 percent of the proceeds going toward food security and access to education. Moreover, this year saw the creation of the Hope Blooms alumni network, which will include those who are at the university level, each of whom will be assigned to youth three to four years younger to mentor. Hope Blooms Alumni are responsible for giving university advice, helping with the application process, and giving advice on the transition. Additionally, we developed Empowered Women Blossom (E.W.B.), a group of senior women from the North End who are now starting their own line of greeting cards to sell in the hope of giving back to the community. It is important to show appreciation to those that have laid the path and foundation for the current generation to now thrive into. Here is what one of the seniors in our community had to say:

"The elders would like to say our community is the way. It makes us proud to see Hope Blooms has planted the seed. We've watched these children grow from young babies to becoming sisters, brothers, friends, and essentially family to one another. And like the garden, they grow with no colour or race hate, only love for all. In this community and garden we walk together, it is also said that children shall lead. Hope Blooms, it is with great pride that the elders and community want to follow you, for you have shown us what a little grain of seed can do. Let us invest in our community as you have invested in your garden and education. The Empowered Women Blossom wish you nothing but success and all the future holds for your amazing journey. What a little seed can do...."
—Sharon Johnson

Mamadou Wade with elders from the North End community.

Gathering for garden night.

Hope Blooms

In our garden
You'll see growth
We took an oath
That we would water every seed
Every child we would feed
Especially to those in need
Because this garden
Has soul in the soil
Success in the seeds
Victory in the vegetables
And a future in the flowers

Working long hours
We plant with love
So love will grow
Letting the people know
We care
And wherever hope blooms
We'll be there

We believe
It takes children to raise a village,
not a village to raise a child

Our greenhouse is the guide
Starting with the youth
We created a group of children
Constantly building
A garden of hope
Connecting the community
Underlying unity
And how it's essential
To show that kids have potential
In growing
And becoming
A somebody that will do something
Because we're tired of hearing about kids that do nothing

Hope Blooms
Where we plant seeds
Harvest dreams
And feed
Not just with food
But knowledge
Celebrating our accomplishments
Honouring kids
May they blossom
Showing how awesome
They are
Inside and out
This is what Hope Blooms is about

Come into our garden
Smell the scent of hard work
The determination deep in the dirt
Witness glimpses
Of the love we spread and the love we share
Where hope blooms
We'll always be there

–Guyleigh Johnson

CHAPTER 1

More Than a Bottle of Salad Dressing

"You cannot get through a single day without having an impact on the world around you. What you do makes a difference and you have to decide what kind of difference you want to make."
–Jane Goodall

Apple picking along our garden's fence line.

(FACING PAGE) Aicha and Tolulope tending to the greenhouse.

It was in the garden where I learned the wisdom of a six-year-old and saw how a tiny patch of soil could become a world of possibility. Our teachers come in all shapes and sizes, our young people, our old ones, our plant and animal relations, and it is our collective responsibility to open our hearts and minds to what they have to offer. Youth implore us to be patient, a garden asks us to listen more carefully, and when we come together we learn that everyone has something to give and something to receive.

It was on busy youth nights when the garden would fill with everyone from toddlers to teenagers when I learned that trampled pumpkin plants have an incredible ability to bounce back. I also saw how those same feet that did the trampling one year would learn to tread more lightly the next. And it was amongst parents, grandparents, caregivers, and neighbours that I felt the incredible wisdom and strength of the community. I am forever grateful for their generosity.

Hope Blooms is a place; it is a place of physical, mental, emotional, and spiritual safety. It is a place of unconditional acceptance and inclusion. It is a place of laughter.

Hope Blooms is a mindset; it is the belief that childhood wonderment is a beautiful gift, one that must be nurtured and celebrated. Hope Blooms is a family; it doesn't ask you to be anyone other than yourself. It wraps you up so tightly with love that you know you have found a place where you belong. ◈

What is Hope Blooms?

*"When you change the way you look at things,
the things you look at change."*
–Hope Blooms motto

The significance of working at your craft daily, staying optimistic, and eventually reaping the benefits of your labour is an essential principle that can be applied to most things in life. Many people may be under the impression that our story is a flash in the pan after our rise to stardom with our *Dragons' Den* appearance in 2014 for our not-for-profit salad dressing. What gets lost outside of that spotlight is the work behind the scenes, which is not necessarily televised. Laws of nature teach us that the strongest structures are fortified through great support systems, in order to do more and continue to grow further. Most significant to us at Home Blooms is our core values, which we set from day one.

Hope Blooms Core Values

Our beauty starts and ends with empowering youth. Allowing them to grow more inclusively and impact community leaders in a margin-alized environment. With now more than fifty youth in the program, we're able to collectively grow over three thousand pounds of organic produce for the community, grow pride and a sense of belonging in community, and grow a social enterprise that builds brighter futures from the ground up, while never forgetting the importance of giving back to the community. We are creating collaborative ecosystems rooted with integrity in environments that are culturally relevant. Inclusivity and embracing diversity are core to everything we do. There is no sense of division—black, white, green, or purple: you belong. We are proud to say today that a few Syrian refugee families are even a part of our ever-growing family. Collaboration does not only mean involving those in our close proximity. Infinite possibilities, with a limitless imagination.

Our Programming

Hope Blooms's programming is carried out within a framework of inspiring excellence in our thoughts and actions, and fostering culturally diverse relationships that span multiple generations and ethnicities. Our core education programming includes the following.

(FACING PAGE) Garden manager Shaani, being one with the garden

Youth Organic Urban Agriculture Program

Youth learn to grow food in our four thousand square feet of organic food gardens from May to October, and year-round in our greenhouse.

Digging red russet potatoes on garden night.

In this program, referred to as mixed science, technology, engineering, and math (STEM) education, the youth acquire skills in seed and plant anatomy, crop planning and harvest, small urban agro-eco-system design, food-garden design, soil management, plant nutrition, management of organic fertilizers (including composts), organic methods for the management of pests, vermiculture, indoor growth management, designing and building indoor irrigation systems, plant and agro-ecology, and creating and maintaining seed libraries.

In 2016, four of our youth in grade 11 received their Masters in Organic Gardening from Gaia College in British Columbia (they studied online from January to May). All four are African Nova Scotian and are the youngest in Canada to achieve this certification.

Culinary Arts Program
This once-a-week after-school program is held with a Red Seal chef who is a long-time volunteer with Hope Blooms. The hands-on curriculum is created with youth involvement and is based on a first-year culinary institute course. Youth learn food literacy skills, culinary terminology, development of culturally relevant recipes, kitchen and food production management, as well as hygiene and food safety. They learn about creative culinary methods with a competitive edge, developed through hosting monthly community suppers and quarterly "black box" team

"Hope Blooms is not a place nor a face, it is much more. More precious and pure than you ever thought before. It is a unique family, one of a kind. When you become one of their own, difference in age, colour, or culture does not make you feel left out or alone. I have not been a part of Hope Blooms for long, but believe me when I tell you, this family is strong. Through thick and thin, they have grown. They cherish their memories, they even put them on a throne. One day, soon enough, I will say us or we not them or they. I will have two families, both my own, both treated the same, never forgotten because family is always over fame. You will see that year after year and day after day I'm willing to stay. Because this is the family that will be there whenever or wherever I need them, so why not try to be there whenever or wherever they need me?"
–Kareem

Enjoying Cider Steamed Mussels (see page 63 for recipe).

competitions. Youth learn budgeting, menu development, shopping on a limited budget and cultural customs and traditions around food and celebrations. Youth study for and obtain their Safe Food Handlers designation. Each month, culturally diverse guest chefs come in to provide specialty training in pastry, African Heritage cuisine, and to discuss career options in the culinary arts.

Mentorship and Tutoring Program

This is a culturally relevant mentorship program for our youth aged thirteen to eighteen. Shaped by the youths' interests, it has a focus on developing self-efficacy, strong support networks, employment and life skills, and a passion/engagement in their education. Programming includes weekly tutoring in core school subjects; working with mentors to explore career options and through visiting workplaces and leaders in their professional settings; and leadership development with Hope Blooms–created modules. In summer months, youth ages nine through fifteen are engaged in summer social entrepreneurial camps, and youth ages seven through sixteen in summer urban organic gardening, as well as youth and their families of all ages engaged in culinary/cooking classes and community dinners.

Adding that finishing touch to Crème Brûlée.

New: Flourishing Families

A family cooking and meal-sharing program that will operate weekly year-round. In summer and fall, families will grow in family plots at the garden site, and harvest their vegetables for use in the meals and snacks. During the winter and spring, we will partner with North End community chefs and restaurants to collaborate on facilitation and meal sharing.

Food and Cultural Arts Program

This is a year-round program where youth collaborate with local artists to bring art to life in an outdoor studio at our garden site, and indoors in our new space for the remainder of the year. We will have photography sessions with volunteer professionals and at the end of each summer, host "Seeing Community through Our Eyes," an al fresco gallery exhibit at our garden site featuring Hope Blooms's youth photography. We opened our Viola Desmond Outdoor Theatre at our garden site last summer and had over two hundred community members come out each Thursday evening in August to enjoy a free film. We also had Arabic subtitles added to each film. Our new Syrian community members greatly appreciated this and said they felt very included in Hope Blooms. We will feature community artists from September through to June in an unconventional gallery setting surrounding the urban kitchen.

Youth-Led Social Enterprise and Scholarship Program

This is a year-round program where youth learn hands-on how to create, build, and sustain a social business. The program includes education in business-plan development, financial literacy, customer and community engagement, determinants of health, food safety– and agri-food–based business, sustainability development, and social impact. Once participating youth reach sixteen years of age, they are employed in Hope Blooms. This past year we employed six of our youth over the summer and three adults. Through education in contributing to community development, this past year the youth worked with a group of twelve seniors from the community, teaching them social entrepreneurship skills. They started growing edible flowers to sell at a local restaurant and put one hundred percent of the proceeds into a senior's lunch program.

Youth also grow the herbs for their herb dressings, make the dressings, design packaging, and develop strategies along with critical paths, and market their dressings. They were successful in securing a contract with all metro Halifax Loblaw Superstores and conduct customer appreciation weekends year-round in the stores. All proceeds from the

Food is a big part of my life and my family. There is a certain effect and impact that a meal can have in a household; a moment of connection you can share with loved ones in your busy lives. Both of my parents are originally from West Africa, Senegal, and immigrated to North America in their adolescence in pursuit of a better life and prosperous future for their children. Growing up, I was instilled with cultural values and knowledge of my Senegalese heritage. This was accomplished through learning the traditional dialect of Wolof and having a well-balanced diet between Canadian, American, and Senegalese dishes. This was very impactful because it allowed me to always remember where I am from, allowing my taste buds to take a journey to remember my roots. If individuals consume food that corresponds with their ethnic background, it will help them restore or strengthen their connection with their heritage.
—Bocar & Mamadou Wade

herb-dressing sales go into a scholarship fund for all youth involved. Once youth graduate and go on to post-secondary education, they become Hope Blooms alumni with a built-in support network to sustain mentorship and friendships. Upon graduation, youth contribute back to their community through mentorship and support for younger youth.

New: Inclusive Social Impact Entrepreneurship Program

This program is built around a sharing kitchen that helps newcomers as well as long-standing residents of North End Halifax address a community need while creating an agri-food–based social enterprise collaboratively. They will have local mentors (staff and youth of Hope Blooms as well as community business and organizations) help with creating a micro-business canvas, develop their idea, create their product, provide customer service, create social networks, bring their product to market, and contribute back to the community through food-security initiatives.

Throughout our decade of operation, Hope Blooms has generated a significant impact in the North End community we serve, particularly in regards to tackling food insecurities and forging better inclusion and confidence within the community. Here's a look at some of the highlights so far.

Food Security

- Over the past 8 years we have grown over 27,000 pounds of organic vegetables and fruit for community members dealing with food insecurity, all free of charge.
- We have a small food hub where, on a monthly basis, we serve 260 healthy meals and 306 healthy snacks to community members in the inner-city community we serve.
- We have a farm-exchange program throughout the Annapolis Valley and collaborated in the summer of 2017 in bringing another 500 pounds of organic produce that our youth donated to the 110 Syrian refugees that now live in their community. The youth also donated 15 garden plots to Syrian families so that they can grow food for their families.
- In this past year, Hope Blooms has held 87 food literacy/ cooking skills- training workshops, monthly free community suppers and weekly free soup for seniors deliveries (over 200 soups) for food insecure seniors in the community.

I had the great privilege of working as the Program Coordinator with Hope Blooms from 2011 to 2013 and I still have the great privilege of calling Hope Blooms my family. In my role, I organized weekly educational gardening workshops for the youth and community members, managed the garden and greenhouse, and helped to establish and grow the junior leadership program. Through all of this, I learned so much more from these youth than I could have ever imparted upon them.
—Sarina

Community Confidence & Inclusion

- In a 2017 survey, 100 percent of respondents indicated that having a plot in Hope Blooms garden has increased their ability to provide healthy food for their families.
- 99 percent of respondents felt a greater sense of belonging in their community since participating in the Hope Blooms garden and programs.
- 92 percent of respondents indicated that their level of community involvement has improved since joining the garden.
- We now have 53 youth, 12 seniors, and 35 families (including 15 newcomer families from Syria) volunteering with Hope Blooms and growing food, relationships, and community.
- We share our commercial kitchen, free of charge, with a group of Syrian newcomers, who have started selling their baked goods weekly at the Halifax Seaport Farmers' Market.

Brotherly love with Makye and Maziah.

"I enjoy the different activities with my friends, because before I was at home and bored. I have made so many more friends now! I aspire to one day be horseback rider."
–Bella

Mamadou and Jaden sharing a laugh.

Ja'niah getting ready for the potato harvest.

Karynza enjoying time in the garden.

Central to our activities in the community is our youth garden. From May through October, we engage youth in fun hands-on gardening that instills a sense of ownership of the garden space, teaches the skills necessary to grow healthy food, encourages positive attitudes towards healthy eating, and fosters a sense of belonging to a family-type network of peers. The youth have their own section of garden that they are in charge of planning, watering, weeding, harvesting, and protecting, and with all this responsibility, you are guaranteed to see a number of youth there every day checking on their hard work. Not only do the youth learn how to be responsible land stewards through the direct experience of growing their own food, they also take part in various sport, art, and music activities, as well as field trips that are designed to transfer food production knowledge in a fun and empowering way.

Over the years the parents of the youth have become more involved in our programming, largely due to encouragement from their own children. These plots provide families with the opportunity to grow their own nutritious food in a community setting. Many of these families would not otherwise have access to arable land on which to

"We love our community garden. It keeps our children safe and off the streets as well as giving them a sense of pride, belonging, letting the kids know that they matter and when we all come together we can all do great things."
−Parent and Hope Blooms community member

Na'siya picking swiss chard.

"I am from Nigeria and farming is a way of life for us there. Having my children Involved in the garden, in farming, feels like I am showing them a tradition from home. It feels like back home at the garden and it has brought my family together. The kids eat the vegetables just because they grew them...like back home."
—Mother, garden plot holder, and Hope Blooms staff member

Craig barbecuing for our annual garden party

"The garden provided me with socialization when I didn't know anyone in the city. It helped me feel connected to and part of the community. It vastly improved my quality of life and the people I have met through it have been lovely. I would be heartbroken to ever see it disappear."
—Community garden plot holder

grow their own food. We now have twenty-seven family plots available to community members for free and will be expanding in the coming season.

The garden hosts many community gatherings where hundreds of people come to celebrate in an inclusive and beautiful environment. Summer BBQs, musical performances, community clean-ups, and plant and vegetable sales are a few examples of how this space is used as a setting for the coming together of people.

CHAPTER 2

Hungry for Hope

"It is easier to build strong children than to repair broken men."
–Frederick Douglass

The beat of my neighbourhood and the boom of a basketball against the asphalt. The "poor inner-city youth" narrative plays as we bathe in the riches of the love and hope our community gives us. We rise up in spite of being seen as inferior we're black and proud but also our interior. Watching your friends move out from down the street as a condo becomes your new neighbour. Saying hi, but only hearing your voice echo back. They don't say anything—they're scared 'cause you're black. Freezie cups on Gottingen artisanal cheese, too; you felt so loved, in the mix, but they aren't interested in you. Stopped by the police, followed in stores—sometimes I don't want to live here anymore. But where else does the boom of the basketball sound quite the same? Where else can you see everybody and know their names? Where else can you run through the streets and feel on top of the world? Where else could I hear the beat of my neighbourhood?

Artwork by Black Book Collective.

I live in the North End of Halifax, an inner-city community that has been plagued by racialized poverty for generations. A community known for drugs, violence, and dropouts despite its true, underlying beauty. I live in a society that even today discriminates, marginalizes, and intimidates me because of the colour of my skin. But I come from a country where being black is not seen as something that separates, but part of a rich culture that unifies. In order to create change, you must have the ability to filter out the limitations that society imposes upon you. As a young black man, I can relate to this so much. Growing up I was never that well off, and I saw clothes as an opportunity to express wealth that I never really had. Despite our social, economic, and cultural differences, we are defined by our possessions. Our clothing

Artwork by Folayemi.

(FACING PAGE) "We go to school, then we grow food in our garden, we hang out and we dream big...what will we do next." -Hope blooms Garden Guardian

correlates with the class structure that we try to depict. Therefore, there is a societal pressure to dress in a certain way to escape prejudgment. A driving force behind all this is the internal tug-of-war we have as black people, dealing with the pressures of being looked upon in a good light by others. This pressure is even more daunting when you come from a stigmatized area riddled with poverty.

My race and background affect how people perceive me. An item of clothing can redefine your class in an instant, the wearer can forget their social standing and feel like they belong in the upper echelons; the right shoes can represent a symbol of hope. I have so much personal pride in not looking poor, and this is a general consensus in the black community. Ironically, I first joined Hope Blooms garden because of the honorarium I would get: one hundred dollars by the end of the summer. This may seem small, but for a twelve-year-old, it meant the world, because I would now be able to get a new pair of sneakers for school.

"Music is an art that lets you express who you are in a different way. Hearing the melodies and drums. Music brings out everything about who I am. Making music makes me feel creative and is something that I really love to do. By simply adding a sound, music can make me understand things better. There are all kinds of music that can sound and feel what your mood is. For example, if I want to dance I will listen to pop music. If I want to understand something I will listen to hip hop/rap music. This is my favourite genre and it makes me feel vibrant. I can listen to music for the entire day, with no worries in the world. Music is a part of me and makes me who I am today."
—Makye Clayton

Barb, Aicha, and Raven.

"I dream that gun violence is resolved one day because it affects all lives and all ages."
—Folayemi

Jazaion finding balance of work and play.

"Gardening is the most therapeutic and defiant act you can do. Plus you get strawberries."
-Ron Finley

Minorities are constantly looked upon as poor and powerless, so fashion is used as a shield. We must reverse this way of thinking in order to prosper in our communities.

Regardless of your age, you can make a difference. The youth in my community are making a better future. I want all of us to have an equal chance of success no matter what our ethnicity and the challenges we face every day in our neighbourhood. As a role model to many of these youth, I'm counted on to help them overcome the various challenges they face; therefore, I must make sure I become successful. I need to show them that beauty and excellence aren't determined by your postal code. That the inner city of Halifax is a place of rich culture and diversity and an affordable and safe environment for our children to flourish.

The stigmas of this community eventually wore me down. I felt anger, intimidation, and fear, which are all common feelings in the youth who live here. I had to find something I could grab onto to give me confidence. This is where my passion for being a role model came to life. I found joy in inspiring young people to dream big and work together to make their dreams a reality as a community. I believe that one thing worth protecting in my community is our futures. This intangible idea of the protection of your future may seem absurd, but it's worth protecting and thus, creating. Youth in my community are stuck in the cycle of poverty. I am tired of being a statistic! Born into poverty, barely getting through school (many not even graduating), and then living in the same low-income housing as the generations before. You cannot control which family you are born into, but you can control your attitude from then on. Furthermore, at Hope Blooms we empower our children to dream, to see more in their futures. In order to grow, you must understand your environment. ✳

Just Anotha Negro

A'int I just anotha negro wasn't I captured stacked on top of ships chained with my brothers and my sisters. Whiplashed on my back eating dog scraps. No clothes on our back for centuries we've always been whack. I am sorry if I make you uncomfortable soon as I talk about this seems like I'm holding the grudge just anotha negro but shouldn't I budge? Should I accept the fact that master put brothers and sisters against our melanin skin believed to be burnt sounds like I just regurgitate guess this was our fate just anotha negro....
—Toulope Boboye

Adruis preparing the soil for planting.

I come from a community known for its trash-spotted streets, pizza shacks, and project housing as far as the eye can see, brick on brick, graffiti harmonizing with its curves. Outsiders have never understood the true beauty of my community. I share the North End through my lens, my eyes, a true window our lives. The North End is block parties on Gottingen, newcomers, sun-kissed summers, hopscotch and double-dutch. The North End is Aunt Mica's egg rolls, sweet potato casserole, Gottingen freezie cups, hairspray, and cornrows. Photography is my passion! And photos are the testimony to the true beauty of the North End. Every pixel has a story.

Queen taking a walk around her community.

Anisa and intern Emily riding around on our bicycle built for food.

CHAPTER 3

Planting Seeds

"We have to shift our attitude of ownership of nature to relationship with nature. The moment you change from ownership to relationship, you create a sense of the sacred."
–Satish Kumar

The Sacred Soil

We are all seeds. We begin small, blowing in the wind, first floating, then flying gracefully until we land. A seed does not decide where it will land, whether it lands in an oasis or a crevice of concrete. But wherever it does land, when a seed is nurtured, along with hard work, it has the potential to blossom. Every seed has a future.

When we are young, we are oblivious to our surroundings: what we feel, see, and hear. As a child, poverty sometimes is masked through adventures and endeavours, through the joys of our youth. I remember hot summer days, sipping sweet nectar from the honeysuckle flowers. My memories are filled with trips to the store, buying ice cream with handfuls of nickels and pennies, and running through, over, and under the jungle gym of police tape with my brother. Living in Ohio felt like a tale out of a storybook, as my parents chased the American Dream. But it was my reality. As I grew older, my roots tried to grow deeper, but I felt the confinement of economic and cultural limitations, the feeling of being trapped in concrete. Living in this environment was the catalyst for me discovering and accepting who I am: a hardworking product of immigrant parents, living in the "hood."

At the ripe age of ten, like a plant I was transplanted. I moved from Cincinnati to a small city in Canada I could not even properly pronounce, Halifax. The Uniacke Square area of North End Halifax is characterized by poor educational outcomes, subsidized housing, high rates of drug use, and a largely marginalized population. It felt like we were moving backwards. Suddenly, I was propagating myself

in an inner-city apartment up north. The country was different, but the setting was almost identical. As a child, my level of innocence and gullibility was so high, I believed the absurd tales, like, *There's no such thing as summer in Canada. There are penguins walking around.*

My parents constantly reminded me and my siblings about the importance of family and community. I later realized how profoundly true their words were.

While walking from school one day, I decided to take a different path home. That moment changed my life forever. Having lived all my life stuck in soil labelled concrete, having sprouted in the dark, I finally felt what it was to see the sun. A young bald kid filled with ambition wearing an oversized T-shirt and Rocawear jeans, I was enrolled at St. Patrick's–Alexandra School, and some of my classmates would go to the community garden after school.

Outside the doors of Saint Patricks Alexandra School.

Rather than going straight down the familiar rocky parking lot, I turned left near the park. As I walked further, like an oasis within the desert, a forest of petals, fruits, and vegetables emerged, painting a mosaic of colours in the distance. Even though gardening is not necessarily my passion, the entrepreneurial aspect intrigued me. At this time, I also met with the founder of project, Jessie Jollymore, and realized that I could be a leader in this community by being a role model and instilling confidence in youth by helping them think about how to make a difference. It was a garden named Hope Blooms.

As I walked into the garden I was handed a shovel, so of course I started digging. Gardening became my escape from violence, drugs, and deprivation; my shovel was my weapon of choice and beautifying the soil was my graffiti. I saw beauty in my community that I had never been privy to. At Hope Blooms, gardening is at our roots. We use gardening as a change agent. I learned that one man can plant a tree, but you need a community to grow a forest. As I grew alongside the garden, I developed as a community leader. Though transplanted into another country, I was able to flourish and blossom. ❀

Shaani Singh.

"You are not Atlas carrying the world on your shoulder. It is good to remember that the planet is carrying you."—Vandana Shiva

Humble Beginnings…And Still Humble

As a health team assistant at the North End Community Health Centre, I worked with Jessie often, supporting the holistic nutrition programs she delivered in the community. We were a travelling road show, delivering sessions in pockets of the North End wherever community space could be offered, a kitchen was available, and food security was an issue. Jessie was always able to meet people where they were in life and offer innovative solutions customizable to less-advantageous environments, always keeping the social determinants of health at the forefront.

One day I was sitting at my desk and Jessie shared with me an idea she had. A typical interaction with Jessie and I would go like this:
Jessie: [*Fantastic, innovative, out-of-the-box idea*] What do you think?
Me: Sounds great! [*Logistical questions, such as who, what, why, when, where, how much?*]
Jessie: Not sure yet!
Me: [*Shrugs*] We'll figure it out. I'm in!

This conversation was no different. Jessie explained there was an old chunk of the local park that was once a garden but had long since been neglected. She asked me if I'd be interested in helping develop a program centred around youth in the community, with an entrepreneurial component. Some of my who, what, why, where, how questions were already half answered, but it would take us ten-plus years to really figure it out, growing along the way from a program to an organization.

We had a rocky start, pun intended. The garden was a mess. Huge rocks and debris everywhere, four-foot-deep weeds, years of garbage and overgrowth, politics to navigate. Neither Jessie nor I were gardeners or entrepreneurs. But we were blessed to be surrounded by passionate people, and always made sure our team was comprised of representatives of the community, and youth most importantly. Our team had growing pains. As with most projects, everyone had ideas to contribute and sometimes they didn't align with the greater vision. When there is something beautiful and everyone wants a piece of it, things can get uneasy. This can cause setbacks, anger, heartbreak, and conflict. It was through these experiences that we developed into what we are today.

Growing a biodiverse garden that celebrates the diversity of our community.

To recruit, we went around to a few partnering organizations and schools in the catchment area to promote what we were doing. Our most successful membership recruitment initiative was just by being in the

Jill's baby shower in the garden.

garden while kids were playing outside. They'd come by and I'd give them a shovel and snacks, and they'd participate in various activities around gardening. Luckily kids like playing in the dirt! We hosted community events and I started doing regular garden nights once a week, then twice a week. At that time we had around five to twelve youth members off and on. Zachary had a big red wagon that we used to haul veggies, and with that as our float we entered in a local parade that first year, 2008, as the North End Community Garden.

With the garden being in an impoverished, marginalized neigh-bourhood, I witnessed, and was a part of, aspects of some kids' lives that shifted my perspective and had a deep impact on me. Jessie and I both had messy childhoods, and it was a blessing to have the opportunity to provide some support and positivity to kids with similar struggles, who in turn provided us with profound inspiration and motivation. We tried to foster an environment where youth can flourish and develop appetites for positive change through mentorship and experience. ✿

The first time I turned over the soil in the Hope Blooms garden was like cutting into the most beautiful mocha chocolate cake. The garden was in its seventh year of growing and you could feel the nutrients that made up the ground we would grow food upon, the sacred soil. You may question why the soil is so sacred. For many of us it's just dirt. But when you start really connecting to where your food is coming from, there's no way not to acknowledge the soil.

For centuries land has been our livelihood, our medicine, our daily practice of coexistence. Through colonization and the green revolution, traditional and Indigenous communities and practices have been pushed to the sidelines. Away from health and biodiversity, towards greed and control.

Just because something is taken from us, like our connection to the land, doesn't mean it isn't there.

Bringing youth to the seed, to the soil, to the root, is what grows our connection to the earth. In the garden we honour the fact that we are on unceded Mi'kmaw territory, opening and closing each season with a smudging ceremony performed by the elders of our community.

Holding a fistful of soil in our hands, we are not only carrying the past and present, but also our future. The place that will keep us well, if cared for properly. The place we shall return to when our time is done.

We are moving towards a relationship with our food systems that no longer knows what real food looks, feels, or tastes like. We now justify chemicals on our crops and in the environment, while creating major hoops for organic practitioners to jump through. By connecting to the soil, we connect to ourselves.

Our very first harvest season was a bumper crop, thanks to the work of volunteers, kids who helped us plant, and beginner's luck. Our first entrepreneurial venture was salsa, using produce from the garden. Not the smoothest recipe to make! We had kids getting jalapeno juice in their eyes, tomatoes were rotting in bins under our desks, and we were scooping tomato guts out with the kids after school into the evenings. There were many late nights (and still are). We sold our jars of salsa at community events. We teamed up with the Black Business Initiative

Jessie and Makye having fun at the gala.

to offer "business school" to the kids as a summer camp. We hosted
farmers' markets at the garden and always made sure to send free
veggies home with the kids to their families whenever we could.

Thankfully, after a couple years, Jessie had the idea to switch to salad
dressings, and after much brainstorming she coined the name "Hope
Blooms." Now we are now in our tenth year and business is booming.
We always made food security, mentorship, leadership, and giving back
a strong component of what we did. Now we have programming in
these areas almost every day after school, and over fifty kids involved.

Jessie has been one of my greatest mentors and she has impacted my growth as much as the kids involved in this project have. They say life's greatest lessons are learned through our mistakes, and I have learned some of my greatest lessons through Hope Blooms. How to be vulnerable to failure, when to take advice, and that goals can be accomplished no matter how hard it gets if you surround yourself with the right people with the right attitudes.

"You must be the change you wish to see in the world" -Mahatma Gandhi

When I think of our beginning I mostly remember how much we laughed and cried over the hurdles, and the support the vision had. It's a warm feeling. Kids have come and gone as their lives transitioned, some we have been lucky to have since the beginning, and newcomers help keep us fresh and relevant. The space of Hope Blooms was created, and a community came together to make the space feel like a home. ✿

We are guerrilla gardeners. Gardening is our fight. In our arsenal, we are equipped with shovels, seeds, and our most powerful weapon: hope. To be able to feel the cool soil between my toes, to smell fresh raindrops

Maziah ready to eat some cherry tomatoes.

on petals and to hear the excitement of kids picking vegetables, to see the colour of zucchini flowers mid-July: a garden is more than a patch of plants, its home.

If you ever decide to one day walk down the sidewalk on Brunswick Street in Halifax, you will see us, a plant with roots tangled in concrete, my stem crowned with a small bud, ready to blossom into its true potential.

Making preserves for winter and to share with community.

Community harvest giveaway with Queen, Anisa, and Aicha.

CHAPTER 4

Recipes From Our Global Kitchen

"Food is not just fuel. Food is about family, food is about community, food is about identity. And we nourish all those things when we eat well."
—Michael Pollan

Farm trip, 2017.

Food is the problem and food is the solution! In my opinion, food is the most powerful currency and many of our global issues arise from growing food. In California, agricultural water consumption is one of the most evident roots of the drought. In West Africa, the starvation in many children is due to improper distribution of food. In Brazil, the raising of cattle is causing a huge rise in global warming. We have to change the way we look at growing food and that starts within our own communities.

Food is the one true universal language. We hear it all the time, yet do we stop to consider its meaning? No matter your culture, your age, your gender, your socioeconomic status, or your postal code, we all need to eat! I have always loved the idea of bringing people together; I think it is the reason I chose to become a chef. The idea of people coming together around the food I've prepared is a pure and simple joy. It is a gift to come to work at Hope Blooms and pass my passion onto our youth and community. Every week we cook together, eat together, and talk about everything and anything. We play music, dance around the kitchen, and share our ideas to create wonderful flavours. We learn about different cultures and food trends, push each other to grow with friendly compe-titions, and share our food love with our families and community. And as our youth graduate and bring their gifts to the world, I always feel a warm sense of pride that they leave with a passion for food knowledge, and for cooking fearlessly.

In this time of technology, it's harder to come together and be truly present in the moment. Food is the one thing that holds the power to do this, when you make a conscious effort. At Hope Blooms we make sure to do this each day. We come together and nourish our bodies while we nourish our minds and creative spirits, and offer each other our attention and support. Some days it's a three-course fine-dining experience and others it's a takeout pizza. Over the years I've come to realize it's not always about what's on the table but the people around it. ✿

Tash, always making sure everyone's hearts and bellies are full.

Appetizers

Bacon and Egg Salad Serves 6

This is a breakfast-inspired salad with all the taste of bacon, eggs, and toast but with the addition of spinach, so you can serve it up any time of the day.

Croutons
2 cups sourdough bread, cubed
3 tbsp. butter, melted (or bacon fat)
1 tbsp. fresh thyme (or 1 tsp dried)
1/2 tsp. sea salt and pepper

Vinaigrette
2 garlic cloves, halved
3 shallots, sliced
1 tbsp. thyme (or 1 tsp dried)
1/2 cup Extra Virgin Olive Oil
1/4 cup red wine vinegar
1 tbsp. Dijon mustard
1 tbsp. maple syrup
1/2 tsp. sea salt and fresh pepper

Salad
1 lb. spinach
8–12 slices bacon (turkey or coconut bacon also work)
6 eggs

• Preheat the oven to 375°F, and line a baking sheet with parchment
  paper. Toss the bread with the melted butter, thyme, salt, and pepper.
  Spread evenly on the baking sheet and bake for 15–20 minutes or until
  golden.

• Slice the bacon into 1-inch pieces and cook in a sauté pan until crispy.
  Remove the bacon from the pan and cool. Discard all but 1 tbsp of the
  bacon fat. Add the shallots and garlic to the pan and sauté until tender,
  then add the thyme, salt, and pepper.

• In a blender, combine the shallot mixture with the rest of the
  vinaigrette ingredients and blend.

• Poach or fry the eggs to desired doneness.

• Toss the spinach with about half the dressing and divide among
  4 bowls. Top with croutons, bacon, and eggs. Drizzle with some
  additional dressing, and serve.

Chicken Tortilla Soup with Avocado Salsa Serves 10

We all know chicken soup cures everything! This Mexican-inspired chicken soup will do you one better with its spicy broth topped with fresh salsa: it will leave you feeling nourished body and soul.

Avocado Salsa
1 ripe avocado
1 plum tomato
1 jalapeno pepper
1 green onion
2 tbsp fresh cilantro, chopped
2 tsp lime juice
1/4 tsp salt

Soup
4 skinless, boneless chicken breasts
1 tbsp canola oil
4 garlic cloves, minced
8 cups chicken broth
2 large sprigs cilantro
½ cup tomatillo green salsa
2 green onions, thinly sliced
1/4 cup fresh cilantro, chopped
1 family-sized bag tortilla chips
2 limes, cut into wedges

Salsa

• Cut avocado in half lengthwise, then open and discard pit. Using a blunt knife, score avocado into small cubes right down to leathery skin. Scoop diced avocado into a bowl.

• Seed and dice tomato and jalapeno, then add to bowl. Thinly slice green onions then add along with cilantro, lime juice, and salt.

• Stir until well mixed. Set aside.

Soup

- Butterfly chicken breasts. Heat oil in a sauté pan and add chicken. Reduce heat to medium and cook chicken, turning once, for 12 to 15 minutes or until cooked through. Plate chicken for cooling.

- Add the garlic and cook for 1 or 2 more minutes. Add the broth and heat over medium-high with cilantro sprigs until boiling.

- Meanwhile, shred or thinly slice chicken. When broth is boiling, remove cilantro sprigs and add cooked chicken, green salsa, green onions, and chopped cilantro.

- Lay several tortilla chips in each warmed soup bowl. Ladle soup over tortillas and top with a dollop of salsa. Serve immediately with a wedge of lime.

Cider Steamed Mussels Serves 6-8

Mussels are one of those dishes you expect to find in a Nova Scotia restaurant. This is our version. The cider and pancetta give these mussels so much flavour.

3 lbs. mussels
1 tbsp. butter
1/2 cup pancetta
1 small red onion, diced
3 garlic cloves, minced
1/2 tsp. sea salt and fresh pepper
1 can apple cider
3 tbsp. parsley, chopped

• Heat the butter in a stock pot. Add the pancetta and onions and sauté until tender. Add the garlic and continue to cook for about 2 minutes.

• Add the salt and pepper, followed by the mussels, and stir to coat. Pour in the cider and cover. Steam for about 5 minutes or until all of the shells open.

BBQ Method: Place the ingredients up to the cider in a deep foil pan. Cover the pan with foil and place on the barbeque on over an open fire, cook for 15 minutes. This also works over an open fire when camping.

Before...

After!

Green Curry Seafood Chowder Serves 12

This Thai twist on a Nova Scotia favourite is fusion cooking at its best.
It is dairy free and quick to whip up. The green curry coconut broth
will have you checking to see if anyone was looking while you licked
the bowl.

750 ml clam juice
500 ml water
2 cans coconut milk
3 tbsp. green curry paste
2 tbsp. fish sauce
1 tsp. lime zest, or 3 lime leaves
1/2 lb. white fish (haddock, tilapia, cod, or halibut), cubed
1 lb. mussels, cleaned
1/2 1b. lobster meat, thawed
1/2 lb. bay scallops
1/2 lb. baby shrimp
1 red pepper, thinly sliced
1 cup green onions, sliced
1/4 cup lime juice
1/4 cup fresh cilantro, chopped

• Place the first five ingredients in a stockpot, whisk until smooth, and
  bring to a boil.

• Stir in remaining ingredients and cook for 10 minutes or until the
  mussels are cooked. Serve in warm bowls.

Tuscan Panzanella Salad Serves 6

We first came up with this recipe during one of our Italian night culinary classes; we wanted to try something different. At first we were hesitant about a salad that is half bread, but this has since become one of our favourite salads. We hope you give it a try and love it as much as we do.

2–3 lbs. fresh, ripe tomatoes (a mix of size and colour)
1 tbsp. kosher salt
1 loaf (about 6 cups) rosemary focaccia (or Italian crusty bread of choice), cubed
1 cup Extra Virgin Olive Oil
1/2 cup white wine vinegar (red for a stronger flavour)
2–3 garlic cloves, minced
1 tsp. Dijon mustard
1 cup fresh basil leaves, torn
sea salt and fresh black pepper, to taste

- Preheat the oven to 375°F.

- Cut the tomatoes into bite-size pieces and season with 1 tbsp kosher salt. Place the salted tomatoes in a colander and allow some of the excess juices to run off for about 15 minutes.

- Toss the cubed bread with 1/2 cup olive oil and season with salt and pepper. Bake until golden, about 15–20 minutes.

- Whisk together the other 1/2 cup olive oil with vinegar, garlic, and mustard. Season with salt and pepper. (This step can also be done in a blender or food processor)

- Just before serving, toss the bread, tomatoes, basil, and dressing together.

Main Courses

Butter Chicken Poutine Serves 8

Being Canadian we all love a good poutine! With this we paired our
favourite Indian flavours with a classic Canadian dish that shows how
beautiful the world can be when we work together. For a vegetarian
version we use cauliflower instead of chicken, and a good veg stock.

1 tbsp. canola oil
2 lbs. chicken breast
1/2 cup butter
1 tbsp. ginger, minced
1 cup onions, diced
1 cup green peppers, diced
1 tbsp. flour
1 tbsp. garam masala or yellow curry powder
1 tsp. turmeric
1 tsp. paprika
1 tsp. coriander
1 tsp. chilli powder
1/4 tsp. cumin
¼ tsp. cinnamon
2 tbsp. tomato paste
2 cups chicken stock
1/2 cup plain yogurt
sea salt and pepper to taste
10 cups French fries, homemade or frozen
2 cups cheese curds

• Heat the oil in a wok or large sauté pan, then add the chicken and cook
  until starting to brown. While the chicken is cooking, measure out all
  your spices into a small bowl. Remove the chicken from the pan.

• Add the butter to the pan followed by the onions and ginger, and cook
  until the onions are tender. Then add the green pepper, flour, tomato
  paste, and the spices. Cook for 2–3 minutes and stir in the chicken,
  making sure to coat the chicken in the spices.

• Stir in the stock, yogurt, and cream, and bring to a boil. Season with
  lemon juice, salt, and pepper.

• Divide the fries onto 8 plates and top with cheese, followed by chicken.

Jerk Fish Tacos with Tropical Salsa Serves 6

We love spicy foods and Jamaican cooking at Hope Blooms. You can use store-bought jerk seasoning or make this alternative (although it has been adjusted as we don't have access to the right peppers here in Nova Scotia). These fish tacos with a tropical flair are perfect for taco Tuesday with friends.

Jamaican Jerk Rub and Seasoning

2 tsp. onion powder
2 tsp. garlic powder
2 tsp. thyme, dried
2 tsp. sugar
2 tsp. sea salt
1 tsp. black pepper
1 tsp. cayenne pepper
1 tsp. red pepper flakes
1 tsp. paprika
1 tsp. parsley, dried
1 tsp. allspice
1 tsp. cinnamon

- Place all the ingredients into a coffee grinder and process to a smooth powder. Store in an airtight container or Ziploc bag until ready for use.

Jerk Fish Tacos

1 lb. white fish (haddock, tilapia, cod, or halibut)
2-3 tbsp. jerk seasoning
12 small corn or flour tortillas

• Rub the fish with the jerk seasoning and allow to soak in for 10
  minutes. Cook on preheated grill for 3–5 minutes per side (Or in the
  oven.) Shred the fish and serve on tortillas with salsa.

Salsa

1 cup pineapple, diced
1 cup mango, diced
1/4 cup red pepper, diced
1 jalapeno pepper, seeded and diced
1/4 cup green onion, sliced
1/4 cup cilantro, chopped
2 tbsp. lime juice
1/2 tsp. sea salt and pepper

• Stir all the salsa ingredients together and serve over tacos.

Pecan Flax Crusted Trout Serves 4

We raise trout in our greenhouse with our hydroponic system. Here is one of the ways we love to dress it up. This gluten-free crust works well on other meats and fish as well. For a side, we love the flavour paired with roasted fingerling potatoes and arugula salad.

Trout
6 (4–6oz) trout portions, skin on
1/4 cup grainy Dijon mustard
1 cup pecans, crushed
1/2 cup flax seeds, ground
1 tbsp. rosemary, chopped
sea salt and fresh pepper to taste

- Preheat the oven to 400°F and line a baking sheet with parchment paper. Mix the pecans, flax, and rosemary together.

- Season the fish with sea salt and pepper. Coat with mustard followed by the pecans, and place on the baking sheet.

- Bake for 20 minutes, or until internal temperature reaches 180°F.

Roasted fingerlings
2 lbs. fingerling potatoes (baby potatoes also work)
1/4 cup grainy Dijon mustard
1/4 cup fresh dill, chopped
2 tbsp. olive oil
sea salt and fresh pepper

- Slice the potatoes lengthwise, whisk the rest of the ingredients together, and toss the potatoes in it. Bake on a parchment-lined baking sheet at 400°F for 30 minutes or until cooked through and golden.

Arugula salad
2 cups arugula
1 tbsp. olive oil
1 tsp. lemon juice

- Toss all the ingredients together and serve on top of the trout.

Rise and Shine Burgers Serves 4

In Nova Scotia we have Burger Week once a year, where local restaurants get together to make crazy wonderful burger creations and support the local food bank. One night at culinary class, were feeling inspired and came up with our own burger creation, and we want to share it with you. Warning: it takes two hands to hold!

1 1/2 lbs. lean ground beef
1/2 cup crispy onions
1 tbsp. Montreal steak spice
4 everything bagels
8 slices maple bacon, cooked
1 avocado, thinly sliced
4 eggs
1/4 cup maple chipotle mayo (1/4 cup olive oil mayo, 1 tsp. each maple syrup, ketchup, and chipotle purée)

• In a mixing bowl, combine ground beef, crispy onions, and steak spice. Form into 4 (6oz) patties, and chill.

• Preheat the grill and spray with cooking oil. Grill each of the burgers about 6 minutes per side or until cooked through.

• In a non-stick pan, fry the eggs with some salt and pepper to desired doneness (I like over easy!)

• Place a spoonful of mayo on each side of the bagel. Start with the bottom half and top with thinly sliced avocado, followed by the burger patty, 2 slices of bacon, fried egg, and the top half. Enjoy!

Scooby-Doo Mac & Cheese Serves 6-8

This Hope Blooms twist on a classic comfort food is one of the best mac and cheeses you will ever try. It's creamy and cheesy with a hint of spice. We like to serve it up with our favourite hot sauces and some oven-fried chicken.

8 cups cavatappi (corkscrew) pasta, cooked
3 cups milk
1/4 cup butter
2–3 tbsp. cornstarch
1 egg (optional)
1 jalapeno, minced (optional)
1/2 tsp. garlic powder
½ tsp. mustard powder
1 tsp. paprika
2–3 cups orange cheddar
2–3 cups marble cheese
sea salt and pepper to taste

• Preheat the oven to 375°F. Lightly grease a casserole dish and add the cooked pasta.

• Bring the milk, butter, egg, and cornstarch to a boil while whisking. Continue cooking for 2–3 minutes or until thickened. Remove from heat and add the remaining ingredients, save for 1–2 cups of cheese.

• Once well-seasoned, pour the sauce evenly over the pasta. Sprinkle with remaining cheese and bake for 30 minutes. (Add bread crumbs for extra crunch.)

Desserts

Cape Breton Blueberry Grunt Serves 12

With our incredible founder, Jessie Jollymore's, roots being in Cape
Breton, we had to make sure the Cape Breton side of Nova Scotia was
represented. This classic, soul-satisfying dessert is so tasty served up hot
from the oven with a big scoop of ice cream on top.

4 cups fresh blueberries
1 cup white sugar
1 tbsp. cornstarch
1/4 tsp. cinnamon
1 tsp. lemon juice
2 tablespoons shortening
1/2 cup white sugar
1 egg
1 1/4 cups milk
2 cups all-purpose flour
1 tbsp. baking powder

• Preheat oven to 375°F.

• Spread the blueberries in the bottom of a casserole dish or 6 individual
  ramekins and sprinkle 1 cup sugar, cornstarch, cinnamon, and lemon
  juice over top.

• In a separate bowl, cream together the shortening, 1/2 cup sugar, and
  egg. Add the milk, flour, and baking powder and beat until evenly
  combined. Drop by spoonful on top of the blueberries.

• Bake in preheated oven until golden brown, about 30 minutes for 1
  pan or 18 minutes for ramekins.

• Serve with whipped cream or vanilla ice cream.

Chocolate Orange Crème Brûlée Serves 8

We always get excited when we get to do French cooking, because it means a decadent French dessert. This twist on a classic brûlée is so rich and chocolatey that any chocolate addict in your life will be forever grateful when you treat them to this.

2 cups whipping cream
1 cup milk
1/2 cup sugar
1 tsp. vanilla
1 tsp. orange zest
4-6 oz. semi-sweet or dark chocolate chips, or chopped
2 tbsp. Grand Marnier
8 egg yolks
2 eggs
1/2 cup sugar, for topping.

- Preheat oven to 300°F. Simmer cream and milk with sugar, vanilla, Grand Marnier, and zest for about 5–10 minutes, and then stir in the chocolate until smooth.

- Whisk the egg yolks and eggs together in a large bowl and slowly temper with cream mixture (pour the cream mixture in a slow steady stream into the eggs while whisking constantly). Pass through a fine mesh strainer.

- Place 8 ramekins in a high-sided baking dish. Pour the custard evenly into the ramekins and pour hot water in the baking dish to surround them. Ensure the water comes up to meet the custard level. Carefully place on the middle rack of the oven and bake for 30 minutes or until set. The edges should appear fully set, while the centre is still a bit jiggly!

- Remove brûlées from baking dish and allow to cool for 10 minutes. Place in the fridge to cool completely before serving.

- To serve, top each brûlée with 1 tbsp. of sugar, coating evenly, and torch to form a caramel crust. Allow to sit 5 minutes after torching to set the caramel.

Cheaters Green Tea Ice Cream (Matcha) Serves 8-12

For those of us who do not have an ice cream maker at home but love green tea ice cream after sushi (we love sushi night in culinary), we came up with a simple solution. We have made this recipe with ice cream, ice milk, and frozen yogurt and the result is always an empty container.

2 L real vanilla ice cream
2-3 tbsp. matcha green tea powder*

• Allow the ice cream to soften on the counter for 10 minutes, and then spoon into a mixing bowl. Add the green tea powder and stir to evenly combine. Place the ice cream back in the container and freeze for at least 1 hour before serving.

* You may also use a nice blend of green tea, such as Yogi Green Tea Kombucha.

Pumpkin Cheesecake Serves 8–10

Cheesecake is one of life's greatest pleasures, and this version is certainly something to be thankful for when served up at your Thanksgiving dinner.

Crust

2 cups ginger cookie crumbs (gluten-free or regular)
1 tbsp. sugar
4 tbsp butter, melted

• Preheat the oven to 350°F. Combine all the crust ingredients together and press into a springform pan. Bake for 10 minutes and cool.

Cake

2 (8oz) packages cream cheese
1/2 cup brown sugar
1 cup pumpkin purée
1 tsp. cinnamon
1/2 tsp. ginger
1/4 tsp. cloves
1/4 tsp. nutmeg
1 tsp. vanilla
3 large eggs

• Using a mixer, whisk the cream cheese and sugar until fluffy, then stir in the pumpkin and spices. Once combined, add the vanilla followed by the eggs, one at a time.

• Scrape the batter into the spring-form pan and place in the oven at 350°F with a pan of water on the bottom rack for 30 minutes. Reduce heat to 325°F and bake another 20 minutes or until set. Cool on the counter for 30 minutes and then in the fridge for 2–3 hours.

Sweet Apple Beignets (Creole Doughnuts) Makes 36

When our culinary adventures take us to New Orleans, the night is never complete without beignets. We added some apple and cinnamon to this version and we can never get enough of them. We have served them up at a community supper and years later get recipe requests. So here it is, just for you.

1/2 cup warm water
1/4 cup sugar
1 1/2 tsp. dry yeast
1 egg
1/2 tsp. sea salt
3/4 cup buttermilk
4 tbsp. shortening or lard
3–4 cups flour, plus more for rolling
2 tsp. cinnamon
1/4 tsp. nutmeg
2 apples, peeled and shredded
2 cups icing sugar
oil for frying

• Add the water, sugar, and yeast to the mixing bowl and let sit for 2–3 minutes. Using the dough-hook attachment stir in the egg, salt, and milk. Turn off the mixer and add 2 cups of flour. Once incorporated add the shortening, followed by the remaining flour to form a dough. Add 1/2 tsp. cinnamon, the nutmeg, and the apples. Mix for 3–5 minutes.

• Grease a mixing bowl and place in the dough, cover, and let rise for a minimum of 2–3 hours at room temperature, or up to 24 hours chilled.

• Heat the oil to 350°F.

• Flour the counter and roll out the dough to 1/4 inches. With a pastry cutter or pizza wheel, cut into 2-inch squares. Fry each, turning frequently until golden. Place on a plate lined with paper towel. Sprinkle or toss with icing sugar and remaining cinnamon, and eat warm.

Our Dressings

Over the years, we have dreamed up and tested so many different flavours of salad dressing. Some were fantastic, and others not so much. We chose the ones we loved the most, and now have four flavours of Hope Blooms dressing available. Each dressing is made by hand and includes fresh herbs, which we grow in our greenhouse year-round. Only the best of the best makes it to market!

Here we've included some tasty recipes thought up by our in-house chef, Natasha Jollymore, to give you an idea of how we like to incorporate our dressings in a variety of ways. Our dressings are available year-round at Loblaw locations in the Halifax region, or you can stop by our headquarters, where we hold a few bottles of inventory.

Maple Sage

Maple Sage Balsamic Dressing is a clear Canadian flavour. It combines local maple syrup with the earthy flavour of sage, rounded out with aromatic aged · balsamic. It makes a wonderful marinade for fish, chicken, or pork and tastes wonderful with bakery breads, salads, or as a finishing drizzle.

Roasted Squash & Pear Soup with Hope Blooms Maple Sage Balsamic Serves 6–8

This soup tastes like a perfect Nova Scotia fall day. It takes local fall ingredients and roasts them to create a beautiful flavour that truly is a soup for the soul. Best enjoyed with good friends while wearing your favourite sweater!

1 lbs. squash, peeled and chopped
2 pears, peeled and chopped
2 onions, sliced
6 garlic cloves, peeled and crushed
1/2 cup Hope Blooms Maple Sage Balsamic dressing
4–6 cups chicken stock (or vegetable broth)
salt and pepper to taste

- Preheat the oven to 425°F and line a baking sheet with parchment paper. Toss the squash, pears, onion, and garlic cloves with the Maple Sage Balsamic dressing, salt, and pepper. Spread evenly on the baking sheet and roast for 25–30 minutes, or until caramelized.

- Add to stock and bring to a boil, then reduce heat and simmer for 20 minutes.

- Place soup in the blender and purée until smooth. Place soup back in the pot and adjust seasoning as needed. Can also be finished with heavy cream for a richer flavour.

Alvero, Aicha, and Barb readying a unit of our dressing to bring to Superstore.

Hope Blooms Maple Sage
Balsamic Roasted Salmon Serves 4

This recipe is proof that sometimes the simple things are the best.
It works perfectly with any pink fish and the resulting flavour will
make this a go-to for years to come. We cook this recipe in the oven
year-round, but it also works great wrapped in foil over the BBQ or a
campfire.

4 (6 oz.) salmon portions
1/2 cup Hope Blooms Maple Sage Balsamic dressing
salt and pepper

• Place the salmon fillets in a resealable bag and add the dressing. Try
  to remove all the air from the bag and seal. Place in the fridge for 2–3
  hours, allowing the salmon to marinate.

• Preheat oven to 400°F and line a baking sheet with parchment paper.
  Lightly season salmon with sea salt and pepper and place flesh-side
  down on the parchment. Roast salmon for 15–20 minutes or until skin
  starts to lift away from the flesh.

Fresh Basil Pesto

Our Fresh Basil Pesto dressing is a clear favourite during tomato season. Basil has such a beautiful fresh flavour, and when you add a good amount of garlic and fresh Parmesan, how could you go wrong? We love using it to dress pasta, cold or hot, roasting chicken or vegetables, pairing with garden tomatoes, and mixing in mayonnaise for fantastic sandwiches or a veggie dip.

Hope Blooms Tomato Basil Bruschetta   Serves 10–12

This is one we love making up for Hope Blooms company, or just ourselves. It is the first recipe we created with our dressing and we still love it. This bruschetta can be put together in minutes—and the plate can clear just as fast, so always make a little extra.

1 baguette
3 garden tomatoes, ripe but firm
1/4 cup fresh basil
1/4 cup Hope Blooms Fresh Basil Pesto dressing
1 cup fresh Parmesan cheese
salt and pepper, to taste

• Preheat the oven to 400°F and line a baking sheet with parchment paper.

• Dice tomatoes small and place in a bowl. Chop the basil and stir into the tomatoes along with the pesto dressing. Season with salt and pepper if desired.

• Cut the baguette into 1/4-inch rounds and spread out evenly on the baking sheet. Top with the tomato mixture and sprinkle with Parmesan cheese. Bake for 12–15 minutes.

Veggie Gyros Makes 6

We love this gyro recipe, but these roasted vegetables truly have endless possibilities! We also love them in salads, sandwiches, pasta, and omelettes. Weather you grill them or roast them, the flavour is fantastic.

1 red onion, diced
1 small zucchini, diced
3 portobello mushrooms
1 yellow pepper, sliced
1 red pepper, sliced
4–6 garlic cloves, unpeeled
6 Oven Roasted Tomatoes (see recipe on next page)
sea salt and fresh pepper to taste
1/2 cup Hope Blooms Basil Pesto dressing
1/2 cup mayonnaise
1 log PC herbed goat cheese, crumbled
3 cup spinach, sliced
1 cup fresh basil, sliced
6 flatbread rounds

• Preheat the oven to 400°F and line 2 baking sheets with parchment paper. Toss the vegetables with 1/4 cup of the pesto dressing along with sea salt and pepper, and roast for 20 minutes. Alternatively, you can grill the vegetables.

• Mix the rest of the dressing into the mayo and place pesto-mayo mixture in the fridge until ready to serve.

• Squeeze out the roasted garlic and stir into the pesto mayo.

• Grill the flatbreads or place under the broiler. Spread with pesto mayo, add vegetables, roasted tomatoes, cheese, spinach, and basil. Roll and eat!

Oven Roasted Tomatoes
6 small Roma or vine-ripe tomatoes
1/2 tsp. sea salt
1/2 tsp. sugar
1/2 tsp. fresh pepper
1 tsp. Italian seasoning

• Preheat the oven to 400°F and line a baking sheet with parchment paper.

• Halve the tomatoes and place them on the baking sheet. Combine the spices, and sugar and sprinkle on top. Roast the tomatoes for 20–25 minutes, or until starting to brown.

Chipotle Spiced Oregano

Chipotle Spiced Oregano is our newest addition to the Hope Blooms lineup. The perfect balance of sweet and spicy mixed with fresh oregano, it is the perfect marinade for summer grilling, be it fish, meat, or tofu. It also works great for tacos and salads or mixed into some yogurt or sour cream as a dip or spread. We like to mix it with peach Greek yogurt for a true summer flavour.

Cauliflower Rice & Black Bean Salad Serves 6–8

We see cauliflower as a substitute everywhere lately, and for good reason. Whether you love it or have been hesitant to try it, now's your big chance. This truly nutritious salad packs a big flavour punch and makes a fantastic side or packed lunch.

1 large cauliflower
1 can black beans, drained and rinsed
1 cup corn kernels
1 red pepper, diced
1 avocado, diced
1 pint cherry tomatoes, halved
2–3 green onions, sliced
1/2 cup Hope Blooms Chipotle Spiced Oregano dressing
1 lime, juice and zest
1 tsp. sea salt

• Grate the cauliflower, or place florets in the food processor in 2 batches and process into a fine rice-like consistency. Toss all the salad ingredients together in a large bowl with the dressing. Allow the salad to sit for 10 minutes before serving.

Hope Blooms Chipotle Shrimp Tacos Makes 12

These smoky shrimp tacos will give any taco truck a run for their money. A little bit of spice paired up with some cool avocado and citrus are perfect for taking your taste buds on vacation. (They also work great with white fish or ground turkey.)

Shrimp Tacos

2 lbs. shrimp, shells and tails removed
1 tsp. lime zest
1 tsp. sea salt
1/2 tsp. smoked paprika
1/4 cup Hope Blooms Honey Chipotle Spiced Oregano dressing
12 sm tortillas

Avocado Salsa

1 ripe avocado
3 plum tomato
1/2 jalapeno pepper (optional)
3 tbsp. cilantro, chopped
1 tsp. lime juice
1 tbsp. Hope Blooms Honey Chipotle Spiced Oregano dressing
1/2 tsp. cumin
1/4 tsp. salt

• Dice the salsa ingredients finely and stir together in a bowl. Allow the salsa to sit for 10 minutes for the flavours to come together.

• Toss the shrimp with all the seasonings and sauté until cooked.

• Serve on warm tortillas with salsa.

"My involvement in my community and my internal values inspired me to take action. I created a raw-juice business along with my younger brother, called Liquid Harvest. We created our own recipes, designed our own labels, and use ingredients from our community garden, which we harvest on Friday nights after school with other youth. We worked from the ground up entirely. The two flavours we developed were Glow (watermelon, straw-berries, oranges, hibiscus, and honey) and Purify (apple, pineapple, cucumber, and mint). Every Saturday, we sell Hope Blooms salad dressing and our raw juice at the Halifax Seaport Farmers' Market. We arrive at 7 A.M. and always sell out by noon. All of the proceeds from juice sales go back to the youth in our community, like buying Christmas gifts for youth and their families, and 20 percent of proceeds go into the Hope Blooms scholarship fund. Giving back is not a choice for us, but an obligation."
—Bocar & Mamadou Wade

Smoked Lemon Caesar

Our Smoked Lemon Caesar dressing is a twist
on a classic. We turned it into an emulsified
vinaigrette, added lemon balm and a smoky
background, and kept all the garlic for a
dressing that makes the best kale Caesar salad
we've ever tasted and works great for roasting.

Lemon and Asparagus Quinoa Salad   Serves 6–8

We love using protein alternatives and quinoa is so diverse. This salad has
such a fresh flavour and beautiful colour. We love making a double batch
because it tastes even better the next day.

3 cups quinoa, cooked and cooled (red or white, or a mix)
1 lb. asparagus, cut into 1-inch pieces
1 medium red onion, diced
3/4 cup feta cheese, crumbled
1/2 cup parsley, chopped
1 tbsp. olive oil
1/3 cup Hope Blooms Lemon Smoked Caesar dressing
sea salt and fresh pepper to taste

- Heat 1 tbsp. of the oil in a sauté pan, add the onions, and sauté until
  tender. Add the asparagus and cook until tender-crisp, and remove from
  heat.

- Combine all of the ingredients in a mixing bowl and season to taste with
  sea salt and pepper. Serve chilled or at room temperature.

Smoky Lemon Parm Baby Potatoes Serves 6

These potatoes make a perfect side to any meal or a great standalone dish. On occasion we have even added some Brussels sprouts to the recipe with delicious results.

2 lbs. baby red potatoes, washed (and halved if larger)
1/4 cup Hope Blooms Lemon Smoked Caesar dressing
1/2 cup Parmesan, grated
sea salt and pepper to taste

• Preheat the oven to 400°F, and line a baking sheet with parchment paper.

• Place the dried potatoes in a bowl, drizzle the dressing over the potatoes, season with salt, pepper, and Parmesan, and toss to coat. Spread evenly over the baking sheet and bake for 30 minutes, or until cooked through and starting to brown.

Cranberry Pepper Chive

Cranberry Pepper Chive is our holiday dressing
and it only comes around once a year, so
make sure you stock up when you can. It is so
colourful with some extra fresh pepper to spice
up the cranberries—and the winter! It makes
a wonderful gift, and a great addition to any
holiday table. As much as we love adding it to
smashed potatoes or using it as a marinade
for chicken and turkey, this dressing makes the
best holiday salad out there it was made for
spinach and goat cheese.

Candied Ginger Pecans Serves 6

These delightful sweet and crunchy pecans are a must for our Hope
Blooms Holiday Cranberry Pepper Salad (see page 98).

2 cups pecans
1/4 cup maple syrup
1 tsp. ginger, ground
1 tsp. cinnamon, ground
1 tsp. sea salt

• Preheat the oven to 300°F and line a large baking sheet with
  parchment paper.

• Toss all the ingredients together in a bowl to coat. Spread evenly on
  the baking sheet and bake for 25 minutes, or until they start to brown
  slightly. They will still seem tacky, and will crisp up when cool.

• Cool completely, approximately 15 minutes, and then remove
  from the pan, breaking apart any large clusters. Store in an airtight
  container for up to 2 weeks.

Hope Blooms Holiday Cranberry Pepper Salad   Serves 6

Our holiday salad is so full of colour and flavour. The cinnamon and
ginger combined with our cranberry dressing brings that holiday joy to
your mouth and heart.

8 cups of baby spinach
2 cups clementines, peeled and segmented
1 cup dried cranberries
1 cup PC cranberry goat cheese, crumbled
1 cup Candied Ginger Pecans (see recipe on previous page)
1/4 cup Hope Blooms Cranberry Pepper Chive dressing

• In a large bowl, toss the greens with the dressing, then place in serving
  dishes and top with the clementines, cheese, cranberries, and pecans.

Hope Blooms Pecan Cranberry Stuffed Chicken Serves 6

Whether you're looking for a turkey dinner alternative or just a nice Sunday dinner, this stuffed chicken looks as good as it tastes. A dinner-party crowd-pleaser, this recipe can be made ahead, which makes it even better. It also pairs great with our holiday salad!

6 chicken breasts, boneless and skinless (thighs also work great)
1/2 cup Hope Blooms Cranberry Pepper Chive dressing
6 tbsp. PC cranberry goat cheese
1 cup pecans, ground
1 tbsp. fresh rosemary, minced
sea salt and fresh pepper

- Preheat the oven to 400°F and line a baking sheet with parchment paper. You may also wish to cook the chicken on a rack for a crispier finish.

- Place the chicken on parchment paper and cover with a second layer of paper. Gently pound the chicken to about 1/4 of an inch thick. Brush the inside with the dressing and season with salt and pepper. Place 1 tbsp. of cheese in each and roll up.

- Mix the pecans and rosemary together in a shallow bowl. Brush the outside of the chicken roll with the dressing and coat with the pecan mixture. Place on the baking sheet, seam-side down. Roast for about 30 minutes or until cooked through (180°F internal temperature).

CHAPTER 5

Growing Through the Concrete

"Success is to be measured not so much by the position that one has reached in life as by the obstacles which he has overcome while trying to succeed."
–Booker T. Washington

In order to create any form of impact, you must first address the issue. By empowering youth to make a change, they are more open to cultivate an action in response, once they realize the astounding strength they possess. According to a report published in the *Canadian Journal of Public Health*, Nova Scotia and Halifax have some of the highest levels of food insecurity in the country. From the perspective of a native North Ender, this is a legitimate and serious issue. It's also one that is frustrating, and quite difficult to internalize, mainly because of the efforts made by the project I'm a part of.

"By looking at the questions kids are asking, we learn the scope of what needs to be done."
-Buffy Sainte-Marie

The Hope Blooms program has a youth-led community garden. In the past year we grew about 3,000 pounds of fruits and vegetables, which is the equivalent of 9,000 tomatoes or 150,000 beans or even 400,000 leaves of lettuce to put it in perspective, and all of it is given back to the community, free of cost. With our newly built, state-of-the-art greenhouse donated by Build Right Nova Scotia, we will be able to grow more than ever. There are few places where youth feel they have control over anything, or where they can be themselves without judgment. Hope Blooms youth are empowered to take control and actively steer the program in the right direction. In doing so, they take ownership over their contributions and are able to experience the true freedoms and impacts of their efforts. Through hosting monthly community suppers for upwards of forty people, teaching other youth, parents, and neighbours how to grow food, preparing organic soups for seniors, and donating portions of the herb-dressing proceeds to supporting other community-building efforts, these youth are learning and teaching others that the path to self-actualization is also a path to generosity.

So you may be thinking, why does this community have the highest level of food insecurity in the country? I don't have a definitive answer to this question, but rather a piece of advice: PLANT SOME S**T! This is the philosophy of Ron Finley, a man who plants vegetable gardens in South-Central Los Angeles—in abandoned lots, traffic medians, along the curbs. Why? For fun, for defiance, for beauty, and to offer some alternative to fast food in a community where "the drive-thrus are killing more people than the drive-bys." His story resonates with ours, an inner city community garden defying the odds and producing beauty. And the simple fact is that we must grow even more, and feed more, and make sure our community is well, because it is our duty! Being a youth does not define whether or not we can make change; to create impact simply requires dedication to change. Our efforts are to cut down the statistics of our neighbourhood every single day. Without strong mentors to follow, this does not come easy. So we have become those mentors to our youth. 🌸

I started farming at the young age of fifteen, a time in my life when I felt less hope for the future. Coming to farming was an act of resistance that led me to the understanding that all the large issues we face (mental, emotional, and physical health, human rights, environmental racism, etc.) are connected to food. In all my years of farming both in Nova Scotia and India, I have come to learn that my want to care for the earth through farming is fed by my want for connection in a holistic sense.

I have always believed that for true culture shift and appreciation of preservation, it is important to start young. This is why I have found such a home at Hope Blooms. When I started working as the urban farm manager, I said, I want to make Hope Blooms my lifestyle. That has become unbelievably true and I'm so grateful to be working alongside our future change-makers. 🌸

Jazaion and Erica playing in the community park our garden is located in.

The process of creating a youth-driven social movement in a marginalized community and growing enough organic food to feed a community is a real struggle, and one that we are learning to accept and grow with, just as a plant grows deep roots against the friction of the winds that sometimes threaten its survival. We call it "growing in resiliency."

(FACING PAGE) Kitana & Tolulope

Growing up my favourite childhood television show was *Avatar: The Last Airbender*. In the show, the world is divided into nations representing the four elements: water, earth, air, and fire. When fire tries to take over the world, the other elements must band together. This childs show subtly infused so many life lessons within an entertaining cartoon, like the importance of friendship and coming together as one. Guru Pathik once said, "The greatest illusion of this world is the illusion of separation. Things you think are separate and different are actually one and the same. We are all one people, but we live as if divided." He argues for a world of togetherness, united although different instead of separate. The world we live in today is riddled with many dividers. Our egos are sometimes too big to even have empathy for others. Nonetheless, we are all one people and we should act like it, regardless of race, sexual orientation, or class. Success is not constrained by the stigmas or stereotypes of the region in which you reside. Our appearance and status is just a small fraction of what we are made of. It easy to make judgments on a person based off what they look like. But it is very difficult to read someone's heart and true intentions. The youth in my community are making a better future. 🏵

Brianna in the park.

Summer nights with community.

How beautiful childhood is!

CHAPTER 6

Journey Into the Dragons' Den

There is a saying, "Sometimes it takes a village to raise a child,
but sometimes a child may raise the village."
–Original *Dragons' Den* pitch, 2013

Passionate young farmers; Adrius,
Kayleigh, Taymar, Na'siya, and
Ja'naih.

These were the first words I uttered as I locked eyes with the infamous
Dragons. It felt like a fairy tale, but we were finally here. We were all so
young—our ages ranged from eleven to fifteen years old—high-pitched
voices with the occasional crack, filled with energy and on the edge of
puberty, enduring the typical trials and tribulations of any teenager.
Going onto *Dragons' Den* was a dream of ours, and we were collectively
inspired to write a pitch for the show. While we were not really sure
what we were doing, it felt right! Our goal was to receive $10,000
to build a new greenhouse, which would allow us to grow produce
year-round, with part of the proceeds going to a scholarship fund.
We came in with a modest ask. And though there was an underlying
underestimation of our ability because we were such a young bunch, our
expectations were to get a deal with at least one Dragon.

Walking into the infamous den, my heart beat rapidly in my chest,
but I had to look calm and ready. As a leader, I knew my peers might
lose confidence in themselves if they sensed a lack of certainty in me.
The butterflies in my stomach were not necessarily for me, but for the
team. It was important for us to reap the fruits of our labour. Months
of practicing right after school, hours of choosing the right words to
say and the right way to answer questions: it all boiled down to one
moment. A moment bigger than each and every one of us. There was
sweat and tears along the way but this adversity had brought us closer
than ever before. Without necessarily the highest expectations, we were
undoubtedly inspired.

We came, we saw, and we conquered the den. Four out of five agreed to
partner with us, with a total investment of $40,000.

Brad Smith of Build Right Nova Scotia &
Trent Scholt of Nova Scotia Construction
safety council.

Interior of our greenhouse.

There is a large misconception that the Dragons' sole role is to invest money in the pitches they find interesting and sit back as their investments return. Arlene Dickinson's genuine love for us was not for "show." Her belief in us was unparalleled; she came to speak at our fundraiser gala and mentored us along the way. A friendship before a business partnership. Jim Treliving came to Halifax to personally meet all of the youth and deliver the cheque for $40,000. These are the type of moments we hold dear. David Chilton was the first of the four Dragons to verbally agree to partner with us during our pitch, and he has been a continued support and mentor. Bruce Croxon made our eyes water; he really resonated with our story emotionally because he saw the inspiration this would have on his own children. Mr. Kevin O' Leary was the only Dragon to not invest in us. In retrospect it was very disheartening, but it provided us with a life lesson to carry forever.

Dickinson weighed in on O'Leary during his bid to become a Conservative leader, stating, "Kevin, not surprisingly, didn't give [Hope Blooms] anything except for an utter lack of consideration for what these kids were doing, and why it mattered." Sometimes there is value in investing without the bottom line being financial return, but social impact.

PossibiliTEAS photoshoot with Tolulope and Kitana.

"I know how to grow all the veggies now" -Tyler

"It was a better experience than presenting to my junior high class. Way easier. Less stressful and also less judgmental."
–Christiana Hubley

"It was a really fun experience, after the shows aired our following grew much larger. People all over the country: messaging, emailing, following, and sharing our story."
–Tiffany Calvin

"Looking back," Arlene added, "it's plain to see that he didn't participate because there was nothing in it for Kevin. He only saw how he'd lose $10,000 instead of seeing how he might change a kid's life." It is important to understand this concept Arlene voiced, which reverts back to this you-owe-me mentality a lot of the world holds. I remember meeting O'Leary after shooting and he looked, in a sense, disappointed in himself. As he shook my hand, he uttered, "As an entrepreneur, you'll understand why I made this decision one day." This has always stuck with me, and I do not believe I can fully understand his decision because I am a social entrepreneur!

This lack of understanding and empathy is what drives this world into turmoil. Those who lack this level of enlightenment are sometimes the very people that hold political positions. Moreover, not everyone will see eye to eye with your vision even when you try your hardest to convey it. Nonetheless, it is important to strive forward with those who will travel by your side and propel you to greater heights. Before you believe in the product, you must first believe in the people behind it.

Learning together, growing together.

✡

It is human nature to never fully realize the significance of what you do until someone acknowledges the difference you make. We did not realize how inspirational our story would be to others, but after being on the show we were flooded with supportive emails and visits from across the country. Our main reason for making the pitch to *Dragons' Den* was not for the money or notoriety, but to make our community proud, to highlight the good it holds, and to make lasting impact there. In society we constantly idolize celebrities and public figures because of the image they display, without necessarily getting to know where they are rooted as "people." Through our experience, we were able to gain personal relationships with a group of some of the best entrepreneurs in the world.

From the outside looking in, it is easy to assume our story is all sunshine and rainbows, but there are trials and tribulations in stories like ours. Before preparing for our trip to Toronto, we had a roundtable group meeting where we discussed schedule and the activities we were going to undertake while in the city. One of our mentors asked the group as a whole, What are you looking forward to in Toronto? One by one, everyone shared their opinion, Some would say, "visiting CN Tower," others, "I cannot wait to go to the Hard Rock Café." So by the time my turn arrived I was so frustrated, mostly confused, by everyone else's answers. I thought, how could they think this way? Getting a deal should be the most important thing! Therefore, that is what I verbalized. As a young teen at the time, I genuinely took this as a window of opportunity, and considered it solely a business trip with zero room for leisure. Internally maybe I was just fearful, thinking the activities would be a distraction. I saw it as a selfish act, potentially letting down our community if we failed. But in truth, I was the one being selfish: I underestimated my peers' hunger to succeed.

"Travelling to Toronto, and getting to see the big bright lights of the best city in Canada for the first time was an amazing experience. Also, watching a live play of Oz is definitely a moment I cherish. Looking back on Dragons' Den, *I was 11 years old when we filmed. I remember feeling nervous about what how the Dragons would react. All in all we did a good job and succeeded, by sealing deals with 4/5 dragons that day."*
—Folayemi Boboye

We had fun in the city that weekend *and* executed our pitch, an experience of a lifetime. Bocar, Christiana, Tiffany, Folayemi, Kolade, Craig, Rylee, Mamadou, Jessie, Alvero, Jill, Sarina, Tara: a team assigned the task to represent our community, captivating a nation in the process. A lesson I have kept with me these past years since being on *Dragons' Den* is the importance of working hard, being prepared, and dreaming big enough to involve other people. For a dream not only belongs to you but also to your community. And remember, there is always something you can give back.

"We had fun during our time in Toronto. We even rode on the hotel dollies just like The Suite Life of Zack and Cody.*"*
-Craig Cain

Our solar-powered greenhouse.

"Our moment on Dragons' Den *meant that no matter where I come from I can achieve great things. Being part of a great group of people and seeing our dreams come true. Our journey represents how much we can achieve by collectively putting our minds to something. Although my experience was fun and scary, being national televised for the first time."*
–Kolade Boboye

Gardening, a labour of love.

CHAPTER 7

Harvesting Dreams

"My mission in life is not merely to survive, but to thrive, and to do so with some passion, some compassion, some humor, and some style."
—Maya Angelou

Mamadou, being the most stylish gardener we know.

(FACING PAGE) Aicha, jumping for joy.

This journey of Hope Blooms has been so fulfilling in ways that even go beyond my comprehension at times. I never could have imagined being in the position we are in now, ten years later. The beauty is seeing the growth in the youth. Like a plant, kids take a lot of trial and error in order to find out the root of why. For instance, the plants are getting too much sun or are too cold to fully grow into their full potential. Youth need the same attention in order to prosper. I am grateful to have played a small part in realizing the potential our youth have in this world regardless of the stigmas of their environment.

One of the most important aspects of Hope Blooms is giving our youth access to life-long education. In just ten short years, we have already accomplished so much. Here are a few highlights.

• In June 2016, our first Hope Blooms member, Mamadou Wade, graduated from high school and enrolled at the University of Toronto. He receiving Hope Blooms scholarship, provided through sales of our dressings, and also a recipenient of TD Community Leadership Scholarship Award. Mamadou is the first in his family to undertake post-secondary education.
• All Hope Blooms youth who graduated high school in 2018 are in post-secondary education. Many being the first in their families to undertake post-secondary education. One of these youth, Bocar, has been involved in Hope Blooms since 10 years of age and has said, "Beauty and brilliance do not know a postal code. I want to be a role model for my younger sister and prove that where we live is not what defines us." Bocar is now studying computer science at Stanford University.

- In 2016, four of our youth received their Masters Organic Gardeners Certification, making them the youngest in Canada to receive this university credit. Alvero, one of the recipients who has been involved in Hope Blooms for the past seven years, stated, "I have learned so much about life from agriculture and from ecosystems where every-thing thing from a microorganism to a tomato plant has equal value and reverence."

- Our Youth Council was represented at York University in February speaking with international delegates interested in ways to get youth more involved in social enterprise. Our youth made connections with agents of change globally.

- After studying Hope Blooms, academics at the University of Toronto published a case study on at-risk youth and the benefits of social enter-prise. In 2017 the study was incorporated into the university's Social Finance curriculum. Our youth are credited with this research.

- Dalhousie University's School of Health Promotion has conducted research to measure impact of Hope Blooms on the health of its

Annual farm trip with the Hope Blooms crew.

participants through the lens of the youths' parent(s)/guardians. This research was published in spring 2018.

Getting ready to learn together in the garden.

Hope Blooms has also won a number of awards. Here are some of our recent accomplishments.

- *The Coast*:Gold, Best Community Initiative, 2014, 2015, 2016, 2017
- Oxfam Canada: Female Food Hero, 2015
- Ernst and Young Special Citation Social Entrepreneur of the Year Atlantic Canada, 2016
- Governor General Meritorious Service Medal, 2016
- Lieutenant Governor's Architecture Award for Outstanding Design in Greenhouse, 2016 (research and development for design and off-the-grid materials conducted by Hope Blooms youth Kolade Boboye and Bocar Wade)
- CBC: *Dragons' Den* top pitches of all time, 2016

A Garden of Youth

"victory I taste
fear stays near, doubt looms, but
dreams squash nightmares."
–Mamadou Wade

"Family, friendship, and positive attitudes have allowed
me to grow and has prepared me for my future."
–Tara Downey

A community known more for drugs, violence, and dropouts than its beauty and close-knit families. A community that knows all too well that we still live in a society that discriminates, marginalizes, and intimidates because of the colour of someone's skin. It was in experiencing this with the many youth here, along with my passion for

Watering the garden and keeping cool.

"The idea of growing up has always been a blurry haze of ifs and buts. After post-secondary I hope to become a computer programmer. After my first year as an undergrad at Stanford I have fallen in love with computers and their power. I believe that technology has the power to inspire, and to change the world. I hope to one day be in at the intersection of computer science and social change. I want my work to go beyond the keys on my keyboard and beyond the pixels on my computer to illuminate opportunities and change in the lives of those who are underprivileged."
—Bocar Wade

Kolade at graduation.

creating positive change, in leading by example that spurred my inner call to action. As young people, we are constantly hit with the cliché that "we are the future"—I believe it's time we start owning it! As a leader, I am determined to make sure our generation will lead our world to an environmentally responsible and sustainable future. As an urban gardener, I see the soil as a canvas, something that can be beautified with the use of imagination.

Society has always taught me that I am "just a kid" and I have to wait until I grow up until I can make an impact on the world, that I am "just not ready." As the oldest youth in the program, I feel a sense of pride and humility in mentoring the younger kids, and always aim to do my best to inspire my peers. Giving, for us, is not a choice but an absolute obligation. I want all of us to have an equal chance of success despite our ethnicity or economic status.

Leadership is the ability to articulate a vision and unite a team to a attack goal with tremendous force, a force that is incapable of being broken. Setting a certain standard to strive for. Being the first recipient of the Hope Blooms scholarship was an honour allowing me to be able go to my dream school, University of Toronto.

JAY-Z is one of my inspirations from a musician and entrepreneurial level. Recently I have been listening Beyoncé and JAY-Z's collaborative album, *Everything Is Love*. My favourite song on the album is "BOSS." JAY-Z's verse struck me personally. He says, in his neighbourhood, they measure success by how many people around you are successful. That you're broke if everyone but you is broke. The way I interpreted this is that while you journey to ascend to the top, you must bring people along with you. That if you are the only successful one in your group then you are the least prosperous because you did not insure the success of your peers. In essence this is what Hope Blooms embodies: to leave no one behind, to propel to the top collectively or fail together. ❀

(FACING PAGE) PossibiliTEAS photo-shoot with Aicha and Kayleigh.

Syrian newcomers, joining in and showing us a thing of two about farming.

Watermelon on a hot summer's day.

"I hope to open my own educational institution one day that focuses on the curriculum, not the absurd tuition."
–Christiana Hubley

"The way I look at it is as a relay race: I hope to continue to pass this baton of inspiration to those under me by paying it forward as an example. Surreal to think I joined the program as a young boy and have grown into a young man. As I journey to an important phase of my life at St. Francis Xavier University, I hope to illustrate the beauty of where I come from."
–Kolade Boboye

"I love kids so much, my heart is filled with empathy towards them. Therefore, I aspire one day to become a paediatrician or paediatric surgeon. As an adult I want to voice to society the importance of protecting the ecosystem and for people to stop littering by establishing a group that talks to young teens around the world about sustainability within our ever-changing environments."
–Aicha

"Hope Blooms is like a second family to me. I like that the youth are in control, and it gives me a sense of belonging. In the future, I think I'd like to be a paediatric surgeon, which will enable me to save kids' lives every day."
–Kayleigh

"I aspire to improve areas that are poverty-stricken by creating more sustainable gardens across food-deprived areas."
–Anisa

"Coming to Canada as a Syrian refugee has been tough, but the people here are very welcoming. I miss my native land at times. I plan to travel to Paris and become a mechanic."
–Ibrahim

"At Hope Blooms I feel a sense of family, a feeling like I matter. I hope to improve the education system in the inner cities."
–Karynzah

An Introverted Actress

At age eighteen I still occasionally play with Barbie dolls. As I am writing this, there sit two of them on my nightstand. They are both blond, both unproportioned to real women, both wearing pink mini dresses and ridiculously high heels. I got my first Barbie at five years old. She was an ice blond in a red-and-pink-striped dress with red strappy heels. As they say, "the rest is history."

I still don't know what to do in my life, but there is one profession I always come back to: acting. When I was eleven I was given a Barbie for Christmas. It was not the actress I requested, It was the ballroom dancer. I named her Brooke and I still have her, but one section of her left arm has since fallen off. I also received a veterinarian doll; I named her Coventry, but she still was not the coveted actress Barbie. The next Christmas I got the actress Barbie. Oh, I loved her so much. I still do. She came in a mermaid-cut red dress with a gold bustline and waist-cinching belt. Gold heels, which I often say

"I hope one day grow older and go to university and further my education, and eventually get a good job. Racism is a weird concept to me. Why should we judge each other based off differences in skin colouration?"
–Kitana

"I like everybody. I just want to be billionaire one day, so I can help and take care of my family. Forever."
–Jazaion

Bocar and Barb, Dream Team!

"I love digging for potatoes because it's like digging for gold. We dig deep at Hope Blooms. The more I have dug the more friendships and skills I have made. I hate them but I love them. We are family."
—Barbara

"My favourite part of gardening is weeding; it is so much fun! I hope to become a dentist when I get older."
—Journi

"We stand on the shoulders of all those who came before us. And when we grow we become the shoulders for our younger youth."
—Phoenix

are Dior, adorned her small plastic feet. A white faux-fur stole draped her shoulders. A large gold necklace hung from her neck and seahorse-shaped earrings from her ears. I named her Alison because I think that is a name of a pretty girl, and everyone knows actresses must be pretty.

I do not quite get why Barbie is so negative for little girls— well, I get part about unrealistic body image, but—if you think about it, they're perfect instruments for storytelling. Which is exactly what I use them for. When I figured out I was not that bad at writing I began using my Barbie dolls to set scenes for my stories. I even use their clothes in the stories. I name characters based on them. This is the beauty of them, you never actually have to leave a room to hear their stories. This is what I find so magical about storytelling. You can be in Lunenburg, Nova Scotia, and be writing a story about a week you spent in Saskatoon, Saskatchewan. Which is what lead me to want to be an actress.
—Christiana Hubley

Afterword

This book's purpose is to shine a light on the beauty that resides in my community. To tap into different perspectives but illustrate a story of cohesion and unity. It is hard to express all we do in the confines of one book. We are constantly hungry to make a difference. Finding beauty in the things we sometimes neglect or even take for granted in our day-to-day lives. Dandelions are often just seen as weeds and not worth much at all and they are often overlooked. But, looking closer at dandelions, they are actually medicine flowers and healthier than blueberries for your eyes.

We are now in the process of creating a tea business, Possibiliteas, fully operated by our youth. We want to further break the stigmas around inner-city children because we believe every child is full of their own Possibiliteas. And because, like Alan Turing says, "Sometimes it is the people no one imagines anything of who do the things that no one can imagine."

Acknowledgements

For all that we are and hope to be; for the vision we have for making a difference in our world and making our community proud, we owe it to those whose shoulders we stand on—you have all contributed to the people we are today and to the leaders we are growing into.

How do we thank so many people who have done so much for us and with us. Your generosity will live on for generations as we give you our promise that we will flourish in your honour. Thank you.

To our families, our friends, our elders and our Empowered Women Blossom—we love you. You are our hearts and our North Star. We love our community—such soul, faith, and richness in spirit. There is no place like home. Thank you.

To Alvero Wiggins, we love you and we are forever family.

Each and every one of you have impacted our lives in more ways than we have pages to write.

To the people and organizations who helped us start this, the great Mr. Loppie, North End Community Health Centre, Black Business Initiative, Halifax Community Health Board, Halifax Regional Municipality, Halifax Seed, Rustum Southwell, Mike Kennedy, Janet Cheverie, Roma Dingwell and Richard Donald; Carole Fernando, Danny Graham and team at McInnes Cooper; Dorothy Spence and Nick Matheson. And those who took us in when we did not have a home: North Branch Memorial Library, Leave Out Violence (LOVE); Mi'kmaw Native Friendship Centre, St. George's Church, YMCA, Halifax Backpackers, and enVie Restaurant—your friendship and support were, and still are, the rainbow in our clouds.

To the people and organizations who helped us build environments to flourish, inside and out, including Arlene Dickinson and CBC's *Dragons' Den*, Natasha Jackson and Meg Hallett; Brad Smith and team from Mainland Building Trades, Trent Soholt and team from NS Construction Sector Council, Jon Mullin, Brian Lilley, FBM, and the many tradespeople who contributed their time and expertise to build us a state-of-the-art, off-the-grid greenhouse.

To Leo Cruickshanks and family along with Leo's many friends; Matt Canning and team at GBCL; Starr Cain Ghazzawi and her family; Elvis Mantley, we thank you creating a home out of an unfinished space. To Dawn Boylan and her family of friends who are there for us through the highs and lows: thank you. To the teams at Atlantic Superstore: thank you for taking a chance on us and bringing us into your family. Don Hunter, Steve and June Scarf at City Mazda: thank you giving us the means to bring our product to Atlantic Superstores.

To The Coady International Institute, Saint Mary's University's Sobey School of Business, Dalhousie, Mount Saint Vincent University, Nova Scotia Community College, Jack Quarter and team at University of Toronto, and Caroline Shenaz Hossein and team at York University: you all exemplify excellence in action. Thank you for collaborating with us and building bridges for our youth in a love for higher education. To our many many interns, you have each contributed in so many ways to our growth and our successes.

And to our Board of Directors, Craig Thompson, Leslie McLean, Brent Dredger, Kelly Gallant, Mark Boudreau: we love you; we thank you for being there for us not only for support and guidance but also as mentors and role models.